SINGLE-SENTENCE SHAKESPEARE

COURTNEY GORTER

An Imprint of Sterling Publishing Co., Inc.

ISBN 978-1-4114-8060-5
ISBN 978-1-4114-8071-1 (e-book)

Distributed in Canada by Sterling Publishing Co., Inc.
c/o Canadian Manda Group, 664 Annette Street
Toronto, Ontario M6S 2C8, Canada
Distributed in the United Kingdom by GMC Distribution Services
Castle Place, 166 High Street, Lewes, East Sussex BN7 1XU, England
Distributed in Australia by NewSouth Books
University of New South Wales, Sydney, NSW 2052, Australia

For information about custom editions, special sales, and premium and corporate purchases, please contact Sterling Special Sales at 800-805-5489 or specialsales@sterlingpublishing.com.

Manufactured in China

2 4 6 8 10 9 7 5 3 1

sterlingpublishing.com

Cover illustration by Jerry Miller
Cover and interior design by Gina Bonanno
Image credits: see page 96

THE BARD IN BRIEF

SINGLE-SENTENCE SHAKESPEARE

COURTNEY GORTER

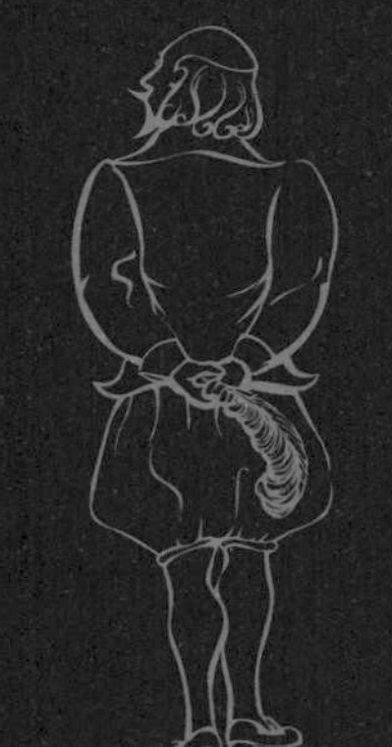

CONTENTS

The premise of *Single-Sentence Shakespeare* is very simple: The plot of each of Shakespeare's thirty-nine plays can be summarized in a single descriptive sentence.

"Sacrilege!" you say. Who would dare to shear Shakespeare's dramas of their pearlescent prose and compress each one's five acts of action into about a dozen words of text?

Well—let's not forget that Shakespeare himself was not above such Procrustean reductions. In his comedy *As You Like It*, for example, he distills the life of any one individual into a mere seven "acts" that take the person from an infant "mewling and puking in the nurse's arms" to the "mere oblivion" of death in just a little over 200 words.

His tragedies aren't any more expansive. Macbeth, in the play that bears his name, reflects how "Life's but a walking shadow, a poor player/That struts and frets his hour upon the stage." That's the entirety of a lifetime streamlined to a single hour in a mere seventeen words. In *Romeo and Juliet*, Juliet dismisses the animosity that has set the Montagues and Capulets at each others' throats for years by disparaging the significance of their family names in a single short analogy: "What's in a name? That which we call a rose/By any other name would smell as sweet." And *Hamlet*? Don't get us started! In his famous Act 3 soliloquy, the melancholy Dane states concisely the existential dilemma that determines his behavior throughout the play: "To be, or not to be: that is the question." All the rest is yada yada yada.

For your convenience, we have divided Bill the Bard's complete canon into five categories that should make their bite-size bits of plot summary even more digestible.

- **Comedies:** Ten plays whose summaries get to the gist of plots featuring identical twin confusions, cross-dressing heroines, and those all's-well-that-ends-well multiple marriages.

- **Tragedies:** Nine dramas that encapsulate Shakespeare's serious side and whose succinct summaries take a light approach to their dark themes.

- **Histories:** Ten plays whose descriptions will help you tell your Johns from your Richards and Henrys, and clarify those confusing Roman numerals and part numbers after their names.

- **Problem Plays:** Six plays whose events alternate from the comic to the tragic and whose summaries address their manic mood swings.

- **Collaborations:** Three plays that show a hand in addition to Shakespeare's own and whose summaries make sense of the confusion that comes with more than one cook stirring the drama pot.

If you haven't guessed by now, the intent of this book is to put a smile on your face as you read our takes on some of the world's most serious works of literature. Remember: Life is short, so plot summaries should be as well.

COMEDIES

Not now, Dad, I see a man who isn't you.

NEVER UPSET A MAGICIAN WITH A TEMPER.

—THE TEMPEST

IT'S EASY TO FORGET YOU'RE IN LOVE WHEN THE PERSON ISN'T STANDING LITERALLY RIGHT IN FRONT OF YOU.

—THE TWO GENTLEMEN OF VERONA

My name is VALENTINE. This romance is a lock!

Surely there are more dignified ways to hide me from your husband.

A five-act play that basically answers the question "Well, why **SHOULDN'T** I send identical love letters **to two different** women?"

—THE MERRY WIVES OF WINDSOR

Having two sets of identical twins running amok could be witchcraft but probably it's just hilarious.

—THE COMEDY OF ERRORS

King
Good lord—
you're me!
No—I'm the
better-looking
identical twin.
JOKER

No wedding cake for YOU!

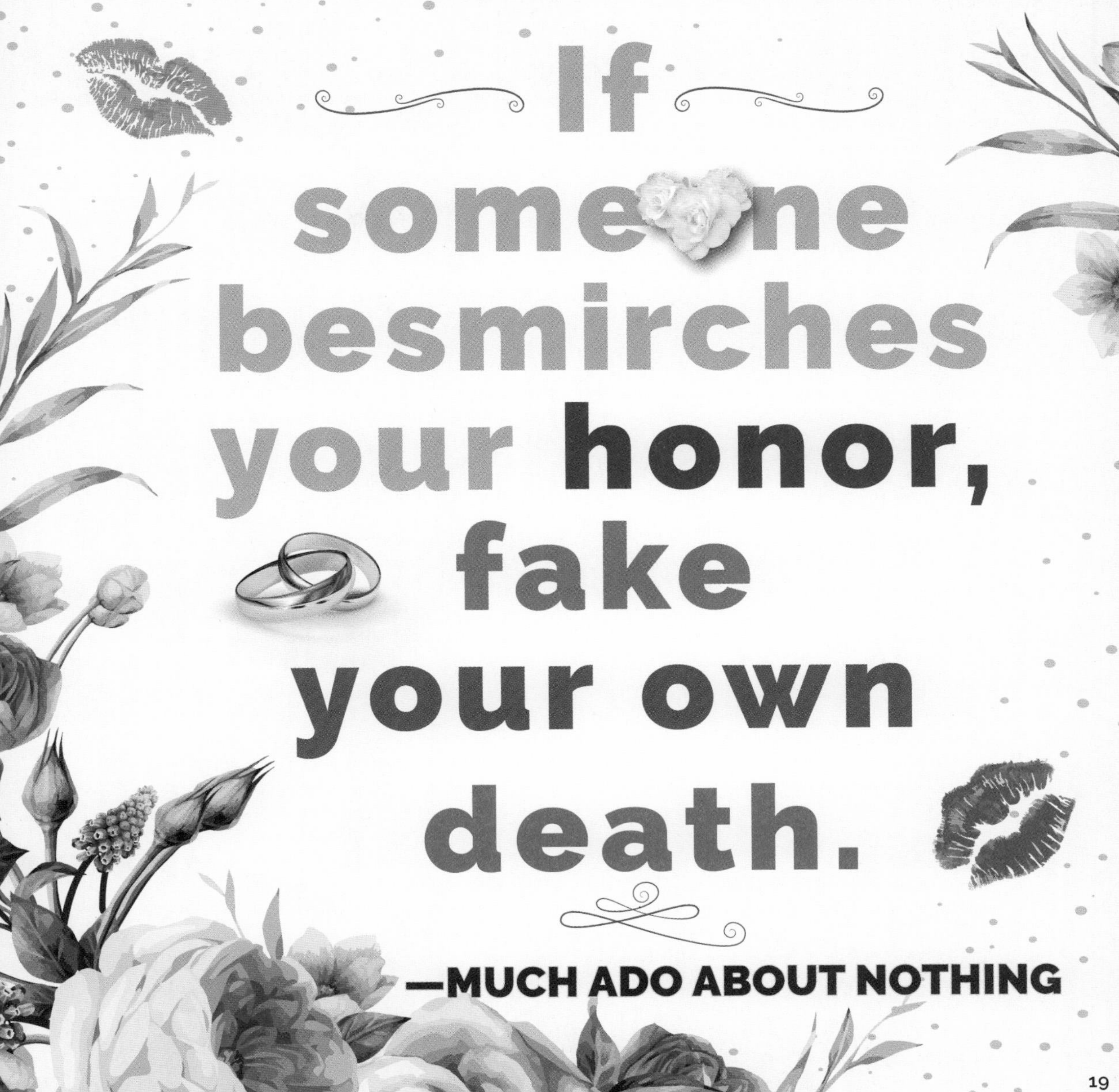
If
someone
besmirches
your honor,
fake
your own
death.
—MUCH ADO ABOUT NOTHING

LOVE'S LABOUR'S LOST

She loves me!
She loves me not!
She loves me!

These four guys gave up dating for three years—you won't believe what happened next!

—LOVE'S LABOUR'S LOST

There's no problem that can't be solved with vaguely explained magic.

—A MIDSUMMER NIGHT'S DREAM

Okay, sprites! Let's get ready to rumble!

Any of you NOT getting married today?

If your friend group is having love troubles, there's a decent chance everything will end in a convenient quadruple wedding.

—AS YOU LIKE IT

Women love a man who marries them for their money and then tries to change their personality.

—THE TAMING OF THE SHREW

If he reads to me in that Elmer Fudd voice one more time . . .

If this is a love triangle, I wanna be the hypotenuse.

IF YOUR STORY HAS A FEW LOOSE ENDS TO TIE UP, HAVE YOU TRIED HAVING A TWIN?

—TWELFTH NIGHT

TRAGEDIES

IF YOU FIND YOURSELF BANISHED FROM THE CITY OF ROME, CONSIDER IT A CHALLENGE.

—CORIOLANUS

EWW, plebeians! Stop touching me!
I never met someone running for consul who wouldn't kiss a baby.

No dessert for me, thanks.

REVENGE IS A DISH BEST SERVED WITH A FLAKY CRUST AND A CHERRY ON TOP.

—TITUS ANDRONICUS

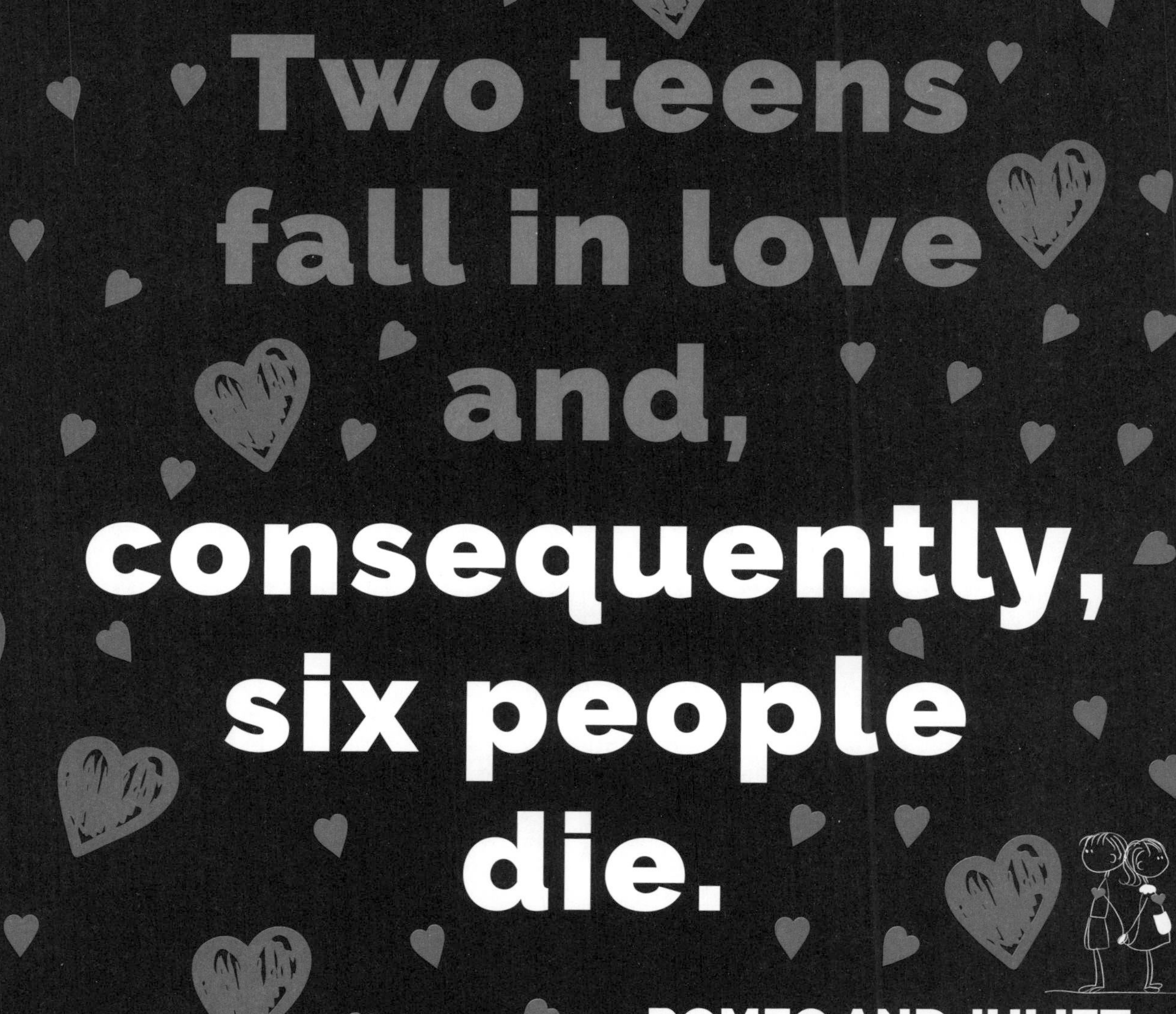
Two teens
fall in love
and,
consequently,
six people
die.
—ROMEO AND JULIET

KISS ME
I love you so much I'm literally dead!

SOMETIMES IT'S THE PEOPLE CLOSEST TO YOU THAT HURT YOU THE MOST

To-GA! To-GA! To-GA!

(WITH SWORDS, RIGHT THERE IN THE MIDDLE OF THE SENATE FLOOR).

—JULIUS CAESAR

Is this the cupboard with the bleach?

The key to marriage is mutually beneficial murder.

—MACBETH

Why do today what you can put off 'til tomorrow

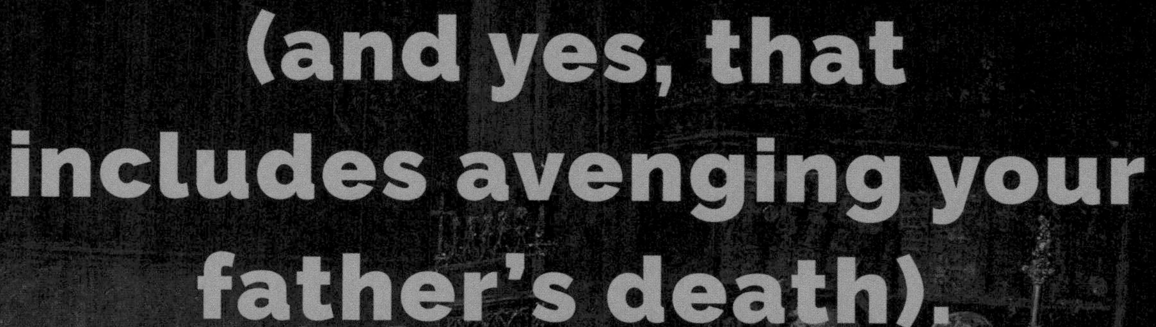

(and yes, that includes avenging your father's death).

—HAMLET

How sharper than a serpent's tooth it is to have a thankless child!

WHEN YOUR DAUGHTER TELLS YOU SHE LOVES YOU SO MUCH THAT SHE CAN'T BEAR TO INSULT YOU WITH FALSE FLATTERY, IT'S TIME TO KICK HER OUT OF THE HOUSE.

—KING LEAR

BEWARE THE GREEN-EYED MONSTER, AND ALSO NEFARIOUS REVENGE PLOTS INVOLVING THE WORLD'S MOST SYMBOLIC HANDKERCHIEF.

—OTHELLO

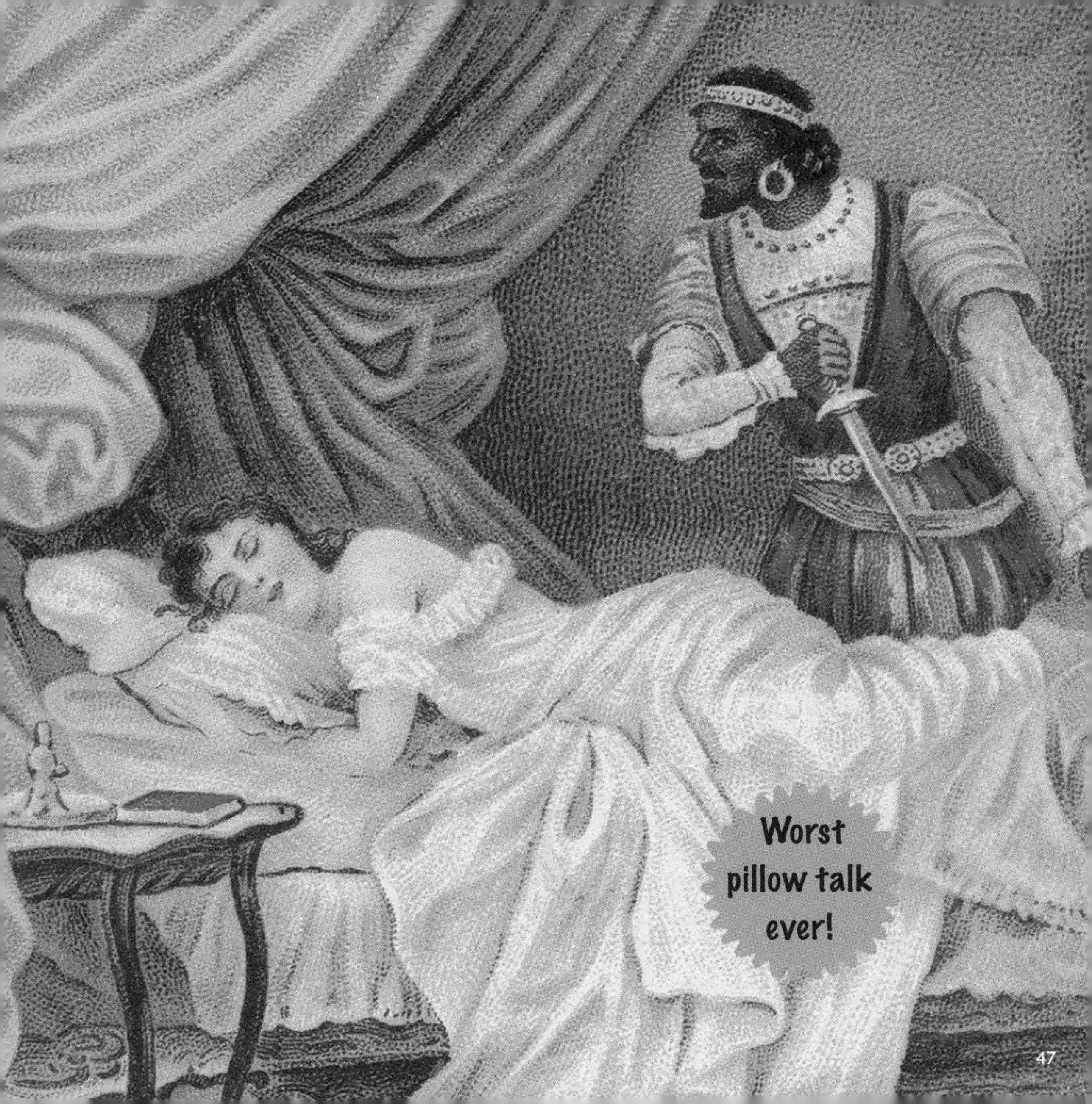
Worst
pillow talk
ever!

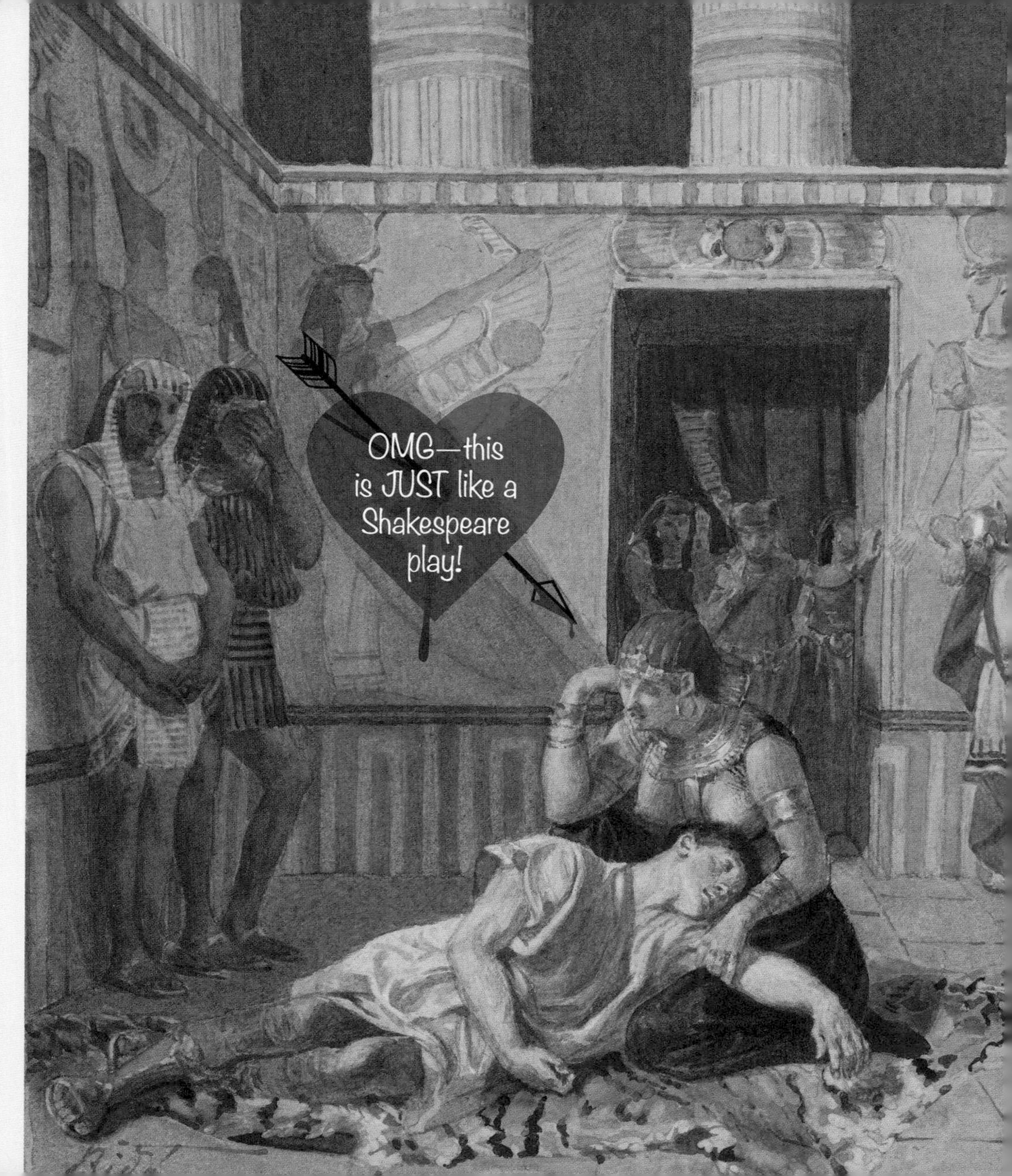
OMG—this
is JUST like a
Shakespeare
play!

WHOOPS, SOMETHING WENT WRONG—TIME TO IMMEDIATELY EMBRACE THE SWEET RELEASE OF DEATH.

—ANTONY AND CLEOPATRA

IT'S LIKE ONE OF THOSE '90S-ERA COMEDIES—AND ITS SOCIAL MORES ARE ABOUT AS OUTDATED.

—CYMBELINE

Yikes!

HISTORIES

MAGNA
SCHMAGNA!!!

KING JOHN WAS THE GUY WHO SIGNED THE MAGNA CARTA, ONE OF THE MOST IMPORTANT HISTORICAL DOCUMENTS OF ALL TIME, SO OBVIOUSLY SHAKESPEARE DECIDED TO SKIP IT.

—KING JOHN

SOMEBODY
SHOULD
PROBABLY
STOP
RICHARD.

—RICHARD II

You did NOT hear this from me

UPDATE ON THE RICHARD SITUATION:

WE STOPPED HIM, BUT AT WHAT COST?

—HENRY IV, PART 1

Dude—now that I'm king, fuggeddaboutit!

UNEASY LIES THE HEAD THAT WEARS A CROWN, ESPECIALLY WHEN YOUR MALE HEIR IS THE ELIZABETHAN VERSION OF A FRAT BOY.

—HENRY IV, PART 2

WHAT WE HAVE HERE IS ONE MAN'S BATTLE WITH HIS INNER DEMONS, AND ALSO WITH FRANCE.

—HENRY V

Go to your deaths, poor miserable wretches!
He does this every time it's his turn to buy a round.

Is this guy for real?
From a thorn comes a rose, and from a rose comes a thorn

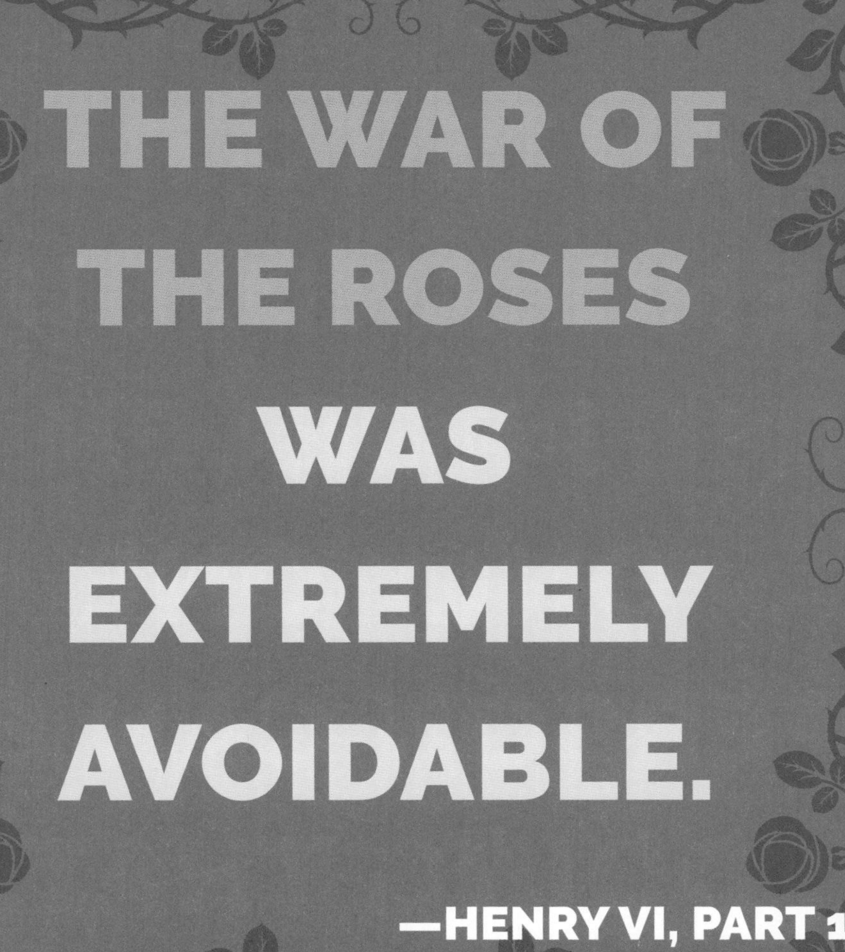
THE WAR OF
THE ROSES
WAS
EXTREMELY
AVOIDABLE.
—HENRY VI, PART 1

EVERYONE WANTS TO RULE ENGLAND, BUT THE PROBLEM IS ONLY ONE PERSON CAN BE DOING THAT.

—HENRY VI, PART 2

The French were the bad guys, but now we're fighting among ourselves?

This is SO confusing.

I can't remember—are you family or a usurper?

SO THIS GOT OUT OF HAND IN A HURRY.

—HENRY VI, PART 3

RICHARD OPENS THE PLAY BY TELLING US HOW EVIL HE IS, THEN SPENDS THE NEXT FIVE ACTS BEHAVING AS IF WE SAID "PROVE IT."

—RICHARD III

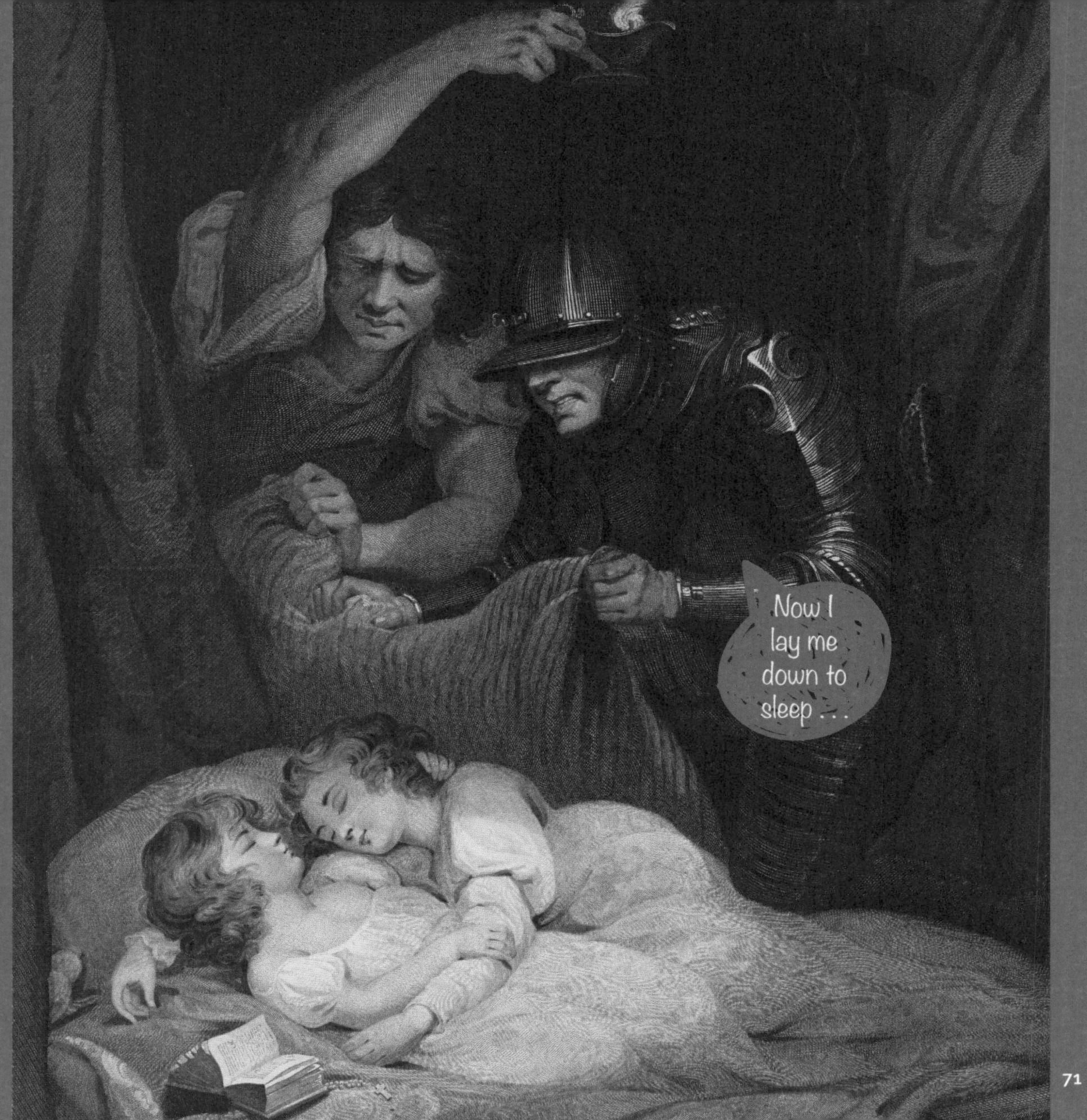
Now I
lay me
down to
sleep . . .

My agent tells me Sam Neill is going to play me some day.

IF THERE'S ONE THING WE KNOW ABOUT HENRY, IT'S THAT HE LOVES PEOPLE WHO DISAGREE WITH HIM.

—HENRY VIII

PROBLEM
PLAYS

I feel like this story has been told before.
Troilus who?

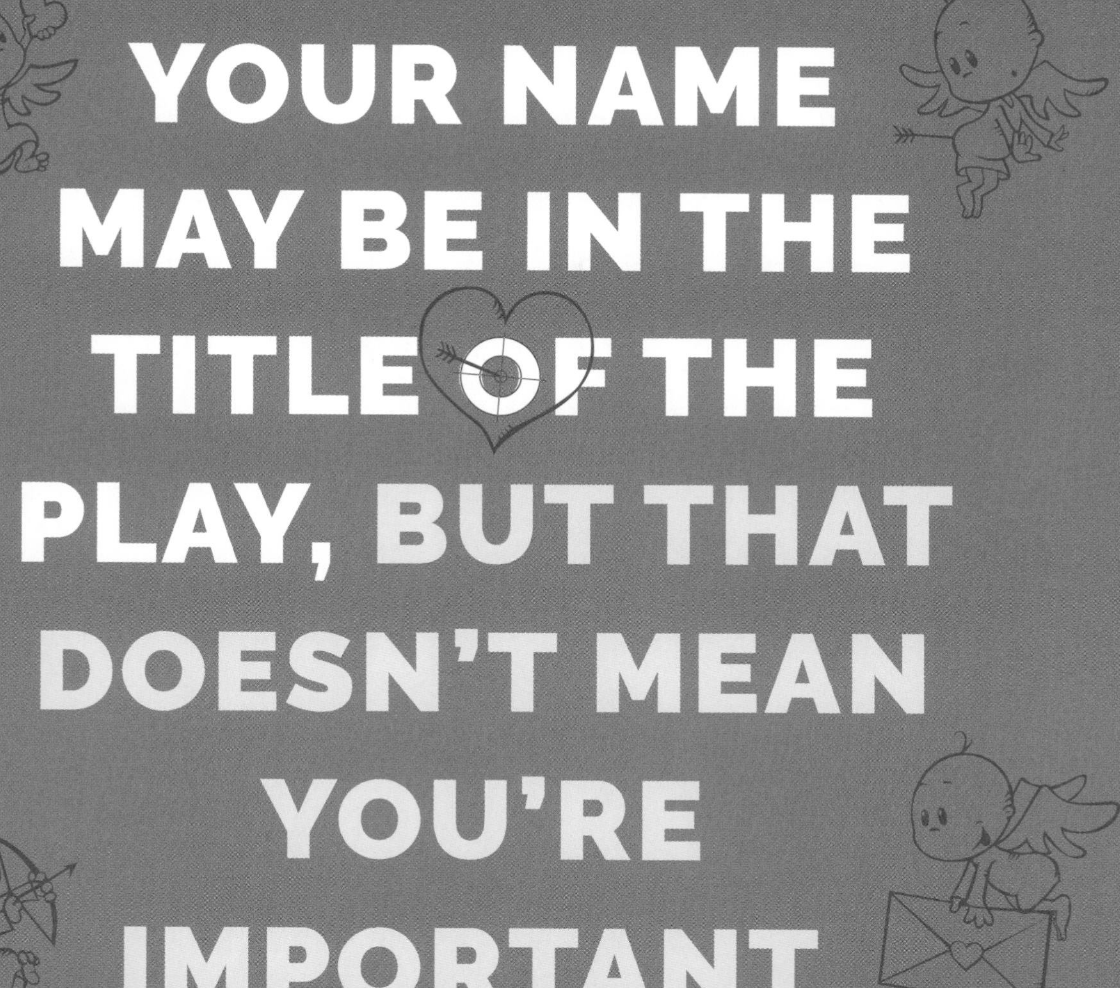

YOUR NAME MAY BE IN THE TITLE OF THE PLAY, BUT THAT DOESN'T MEAN YOU'RE IMPORTANT.

—TROILUS AND CRESSIDA

Sleep with HIM? Ain't gonna be me.
NO!

TRICKING SOMEONE INTO BED WITH YOU IS APPARENTLY TOTALLY FINE AND **NOT** AT ALL ALARMING.

—MEASURE FOR MEASURE

BE THE MISANTHROPIST YOU WISH TO SEE IN THE WORLD.

—TIMON OF ATHENS

It's amazing what gold can buy you

Go away, kids—ya bother me!

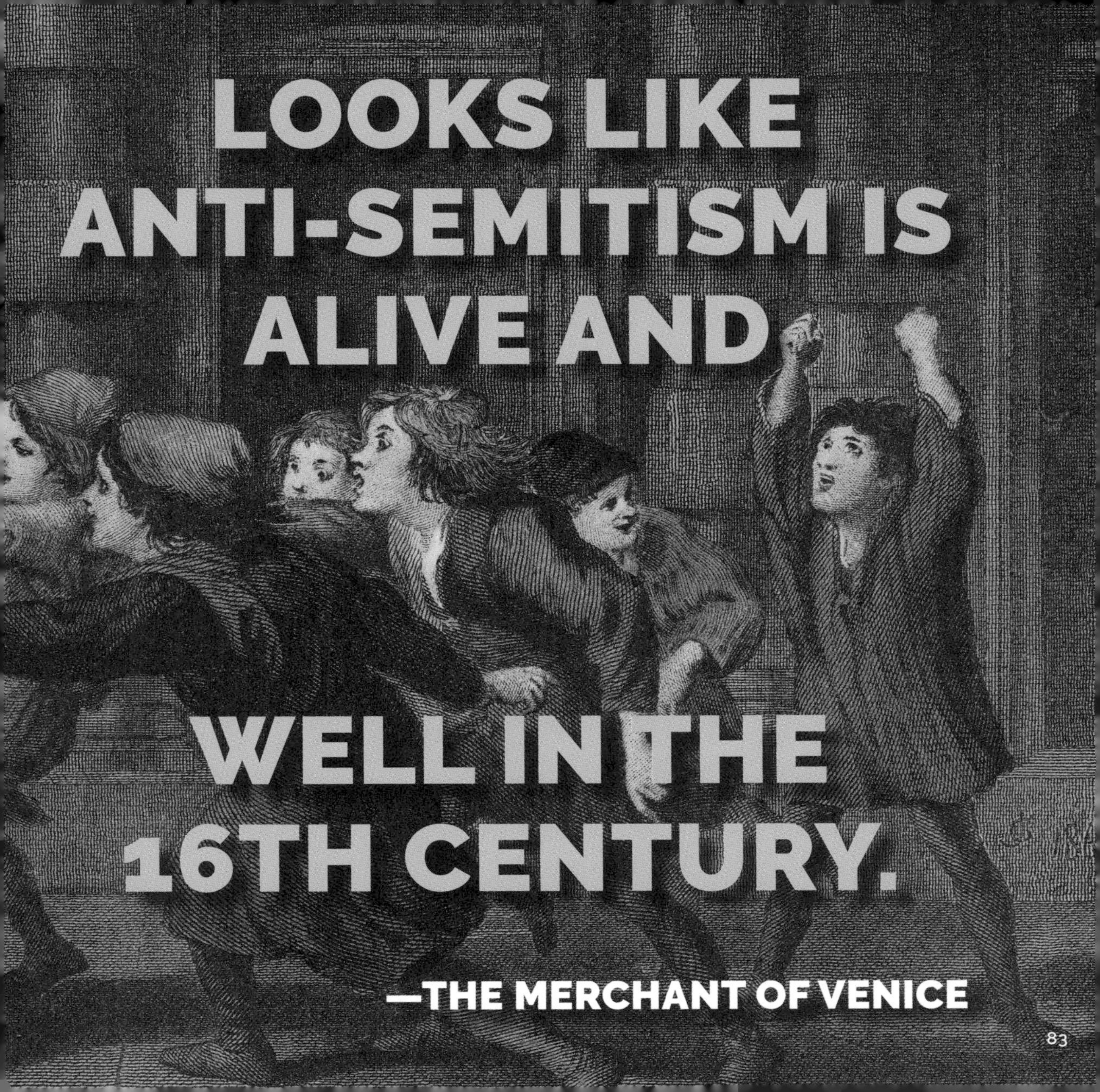

LOOKS LIKE ANTI-SEMITISM IS ALIVE AND

WELL IN THE 16TH CENTURY.

—THE MERCHANT OF VENICE

IF YOU'RE A WOMAN WITH NO MONEY OR PROSPECTS, WELL, GOOD LUCK WITH THAT.

—ALL'S WELL THAT ENDS WELL

You don't know what you're missing!!

Why is mama talking to your best friend?

IT'S BETTER TO HAVE LOVED AND LOST THAN NOT TO HAVE ACTUALLY FACT-CHECKED YOUR WIFE'S ALLEGED INFIDELITY.

—THE WINTER'S TALE

CO

LABORATIONS

It starts with

+es n=r p+ +e -a -f x=f ty+ -d

a ~~riddle~~ and a shipwreck, and things just go nuts from there.

—PERICLES, PRINCE OF TYRE

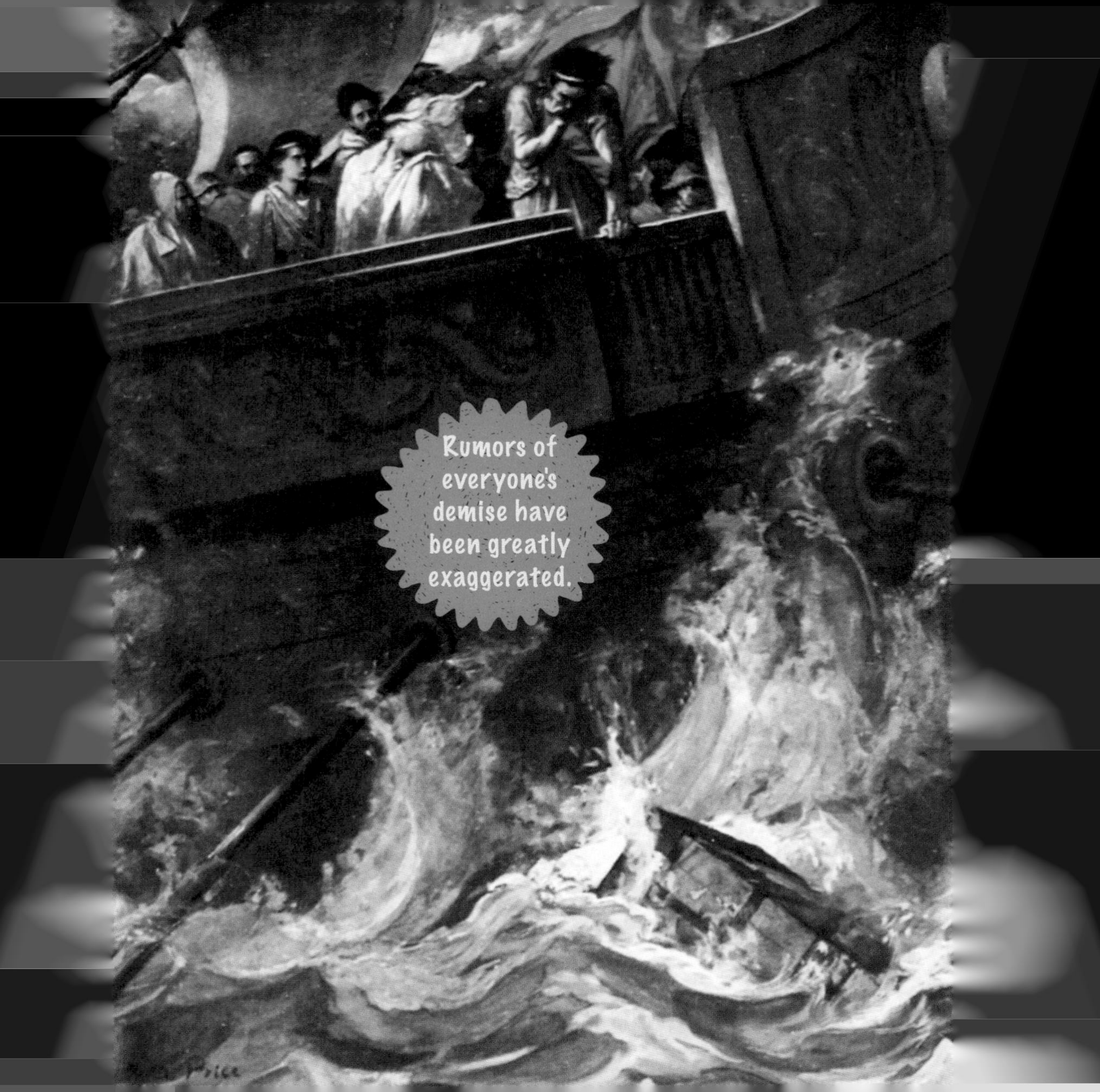
Rumors of everyone's demise have been greatly exaggerated.
Price

One of us is toast today.
Speak for yourself, bro!

FIGHTING YOUR BUDDY FOR THE HAND OF THE WOMAN YOU BOTH LOVE HAS COMPLICATIONS, ESPECIALLY WHEN THE KING JUST WANTS YOU BOTH DEAD.

—THE TWO NOBLE KINSMEN

BEING DECLARED THE TRUE HEIR TO THE PREVIOUS KING OF FRANCE WHEN YOU'RE ALREADY KING OF ENGLAND HAS ITS PRIVILEGES— LIKE BEING ABLE TO SACK FRANCE WHEN THEY INSULT YOU.

—EDWARD III

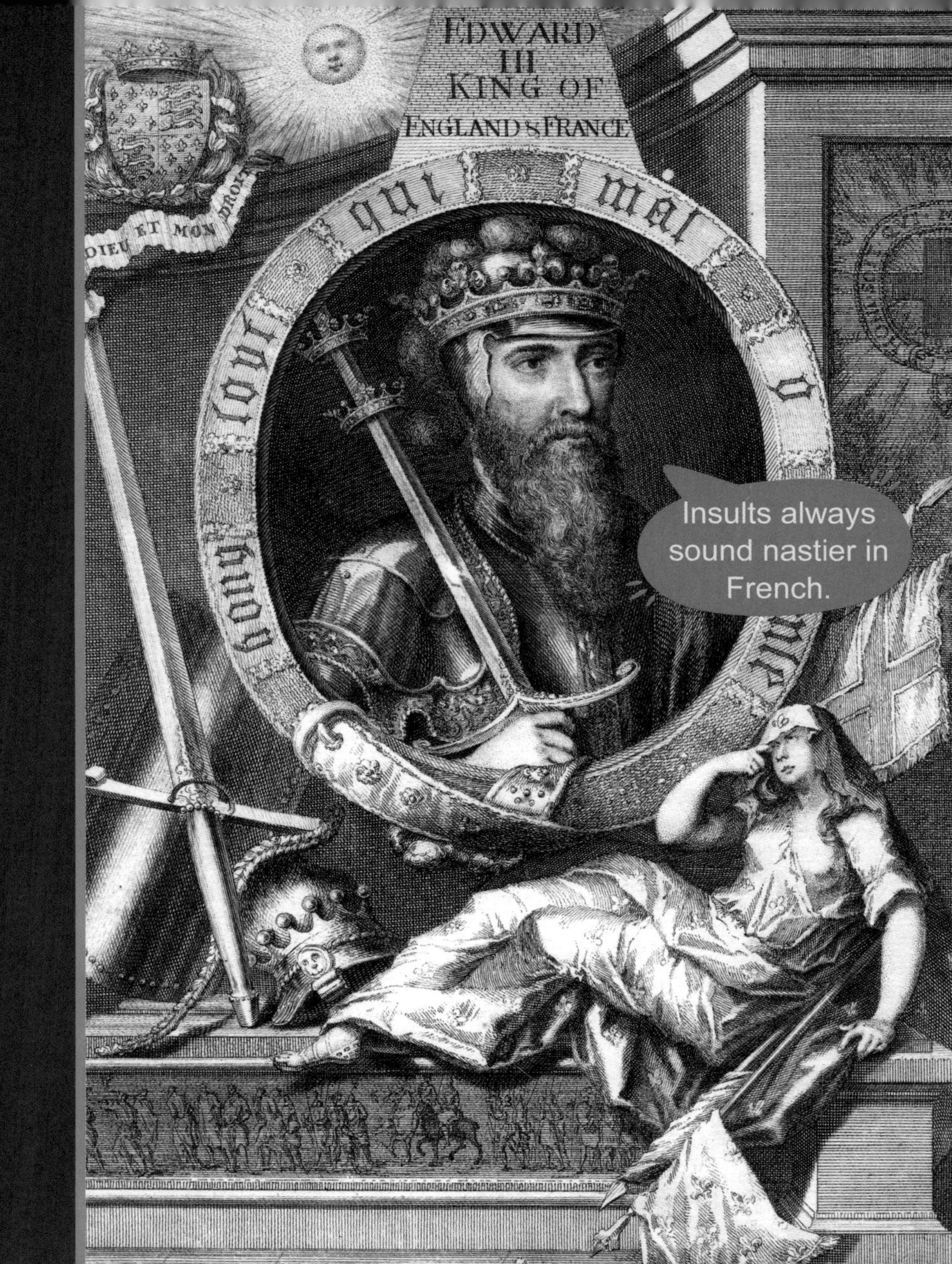
EDWARD
III
KING OF
ENGLAND & FRANCE
DIEU ET MON DROIT
Insults always sound nastier in French.

Akg-images: ©Sotheby's: 44

Alamy: Chronicle: 28; History and Art Collection: 92; INTERFOTO: 14; North Wind Picture Archives: 54; Painters: 27; The Print Collector: 95

Birmingham Museums Trust: 13

Bridgeman Images: 38, 78; ©Christie's Images: 23; Houses of Parliament, London, UK: 64; ©Look and Learn: 47, 91; ©Sheffield Galleries and Museums Trust: 18; ©Southampton City Art Gallery, Hampshire, UK: 37; ©The Maas Gallery, London: 10

Dreamstime: ©Elena Kozyreva: 51

Folger Shakespeare Library: 17, 24, 28, 34, 40, 48, 51, 57, 58, 60, 63, 67, 68, 71, 72, 76, 81, 82, 85, 86

Getty Images: DigitalVision Vecotrs: Keith Lance: 6; iStock/Gety Images Plus: ZU-09: 52; TonyBaggett: 74

Michael John Goodman, The Victorian Illustrated Shakespeare Archive: 3, 8, 15, 20, 25, 30, 31

MUTI: 80

Shutterstock.com: A_kela: 10(rain); agsandrew: 22, 23(magic); Aguni: 20(hearts); Katia August: 37(wings); Azuzl: 5, 7, 89(bubble) BlueberryPie: 63 (bubble); chan art: 54, 85, 95(bubbles); coz1421: 27, 60, 67, 78, 92(bubbles); Kozak Bohdan: 35(pie); dueanchai intaraboonsom: 13, 18,24, 34, 44, 57, 63, 68, 71, 72, 82(bubbles); Efen Guy: 43(cartoon); Ell Mc: 4, 88; ER_09: 28(rip); Frame Art: 10, 13(frames); Alessa Gillespie: 46(pattern); gillmar: 28(frame); HalinaPalina: 19(heart roses); Hardtillustrations: 51(background); Yudi Harjo: 90(fox); InnaPoka: 50(background); Istry Istry: 11(waves); kolbus viktor: 7; lindamka: 90(shipwreck); Filipchuk Maksym: 54(background); mhatzapa: 38, 81(bubbles); mmalkani: 76(border); Mio Buono: 19(confetti); Mirror-Images: 48(heart); Naletova Elena: 58, 59(background); Natalia0307: 17(background); Nataliia K: 35(flies); TINA NIZOVA: 90(cloud); Nuchylee: 41(blood); Ola-la: 19(stationary); olexius: 19(rings); OSIPOVEV: 55(background); paprika: 65(border); paseven: 17(king/joker), 29(waves/rope), 48(border), 49(icon); Maisei Raman: 8(hand); silky: 40(splatter); Ekaterina Shcheglova: 40(handprint); schwarzhana: 77(cupids); Amanita Silvicora: 49(pattern); Boris Sosnovyy: 19(lipstick); Susanitah: 10(ship); Tartila: 61(crown); TashaNatasha: 14, 42, 44, 47, 51, 59, 64, 67, 76, 91 (bubbles); TAW4: 10(lightning); Topilskaya: 36(heart), 37(bubble); Burak Tunc: 10(bubble); Vandreas: 13(room); Virinaflora: 36(couple); Wanchana365: 28, 33, 88(bubbles); ZenStockers: 17(bubbles); zizou7: 90(red dot)

Courtesy of Wikimedia Commons: 33, 42

IMAGE CREDITS